£1

PLANTS FOR THE

COTTAGE
GARDEN

PETER THURMAN

First published in Great Britain in 1994 by
PAVILION BOOKS LIMITED
26 Upper Ground, London SE1 9PD

Conceived, edited and designed by Russell Ash & Bernard Higton
Picture research by Julia Pashley
Plant consultant Tony Lord

A CIP catalogue record for this book is available from the
British Library.

ISBN 1 85793 108 4

Printed and bound in Singapore by Tien Wah Press

2 4 6 8 10 9 7 5 3 1

This book may be ordered by post direct from the publisher.
Please contact the Marketing Department.
But try your bookshop first.

CONTENTS

INTRODUCTION

The image today of the cottage gardens of old is essentially a romantic one This, of course, doesn't really matter: gardens are about dreams and to the country artisan and his family cottage gardens must have been a haven and an escape from the rigours of everyday life – just as they are today.

The cottage garden has probably been around as long as there have been rural, working-class families with a roof over their heads and a patch of land they could call their own. Although gardening was a relatively cheap recreation, the plot had to pay its way too. The result was a seemingly random mixture of vegetables, shrubs, flowers, bulbs, fruit trees, soft fruit and herbs growing together in glorious disarray. Cottage gardens were not planned; they evolved and matured with time, and while they were often very neat and tidy, the sheer density of planting gave an impression of 'organized chaos'.

Vegetables and soft fruit were frequently planted amongst flowers or vice versa. Fragrance in flowers was much sought after; many nectar-rich flowers were grown to attract bees and honey commonly made; aromatic herbs such as southernwood and wormwood were strewn over floors to deter fleas and yellow loosestrife flowers were dried and hung from ceilings to keep away flies. The medicinal uses of plants were widely known and used: prunella leaves, for example, were thought to heal wounds, hence its common name, 'self-heal'.

DETAIL OF *IN THE COTTAGE GARDEN* BY ARTHUR CLAUDE STRACHAN

In the last century the cottage garden became more ornamental. The husband continued to concentrate on the fruit and vegetables while the rural housewife developed her skill and knowledge in growing herbs and flowers. With more leisure time, gardening became more of a recreational activity. Because cottage gardens represented perhaps the most unpretentious type of garden, when, in the latter part of the 19th century, a new 'natural' style of gardening was advocated, the famous gardening writers William Robinson and Gertrude Jekyll instigated a move away from Victorian formal fussiness and encouraged a move toward the cottage garden.

Cottage gardens 'work' because they unintentionally follow many of the fundamental principles of good garden design, all their parts combining to form a whole, with a feeling of unity. Flowers were allowed to seed themselves around. A 'good doer' may have been thinned-out, but essentially left to dominate and thus unify. Paving and fencing materials were locally acquired and limited in range.

The distinctive visual character of a plant or other garden material is summed up by the word 'texture'. The various textures in a garden work best if they are combined to produce a strong contrast. Plants with similar leaf shapes present a far less interesting picture than a group taking in both narrow grass-like leaves and large roundish leaves. In a cottage garden, vegetable plants often supply this textural contrast as an 'aside'. The narrow upright leaves of onion, or the large leaves of cabbage and lettuce work surprisingly well with small 'normal'-leaved flower varieties.

Colour in a garden is a personal subject and no two gardeners think alike. It is generally agreed, however, that under our greyish skies the cooler, pastel colours come alive whereas the hot bright reds and oranges can look garish. Perhaps it is just a happy accident that many of our wild flowers tend to be softer in colour – and it was these that were prevalent in early cottage gardens.

The basic function behind the cottage garden of yesteryear – the need for self-sufficiency – is no longer such a strong necessity. The retired couple does not have to rely on home-grown vegetables, while they, and younger gardeners, may have romantic aspirations to create a cottage garden but lack the time and knowledge to do so. If you want to have a

ROSES, EVENING PRIMROSE, LADY'S MANTLE AND *ASTILBE* COMPETE FOR
SPACE ON EITHER SIDE OF A GRAVEL PATH AND ENTRANCE.

cottage garden that 'copes' with our modern life styles and
all the incumbent pressures and restrictions, it is vital that
the essential ingredients of the traditional cottage gardens
are considered and then adapted for today's conditions. Here
are a few pointers:

• In certain situations the desire to grow vegetables or fruit
may be negligible, but you can just grow them for their
interesting foliage.

• Restrict the range of materials for paving and fencing.
Avoid 'high-tech' new material and designs.

• Avoid too the 'kitsch' pseudo-cottage style exemplified by
garden gnomes, ill-conceived topiary, wheelbarrows or
stone boots full of petunias, wishing wells, windmills and
plastic ponds.

• Keep paths functional and avoid fussy shapes for the beds;
the planting, profuse and informal, will soften the edges.

• Borders should be mixtures of shrubs, perennials, annuals,
and bulbs, perhaps with a dominant colour or restricted
range of colours.

• Applying some basic colour rules can create very pleasing, harmonious effects, but in a cottage garden rules may be broken. Decide what colour combinations appeal to you and experiment.

• Try to create a random, evolved feel to borders. Don't plant perennials in regimental clumps of similar shape and size. Some varieties should be allowed to form large clusters, whereas others can be small 'dots' of which one only gets a glimpse.

• Allow plants to grow into each other. Do not prune shrubs if they have grown beyond their allotted space, but let them encroach into their neighbours.

• A modern cottage garden is not complete without wildlife and a predominance of fragrant plants. Choose plants that have nectar-rich flowers that attract butterflies and bumble-bees and plants that have scented flowers or aromatic leaves (see Checklists).

• Perennials are a must for a cottage garden, but some of the older 'leggy' varieties will need quite a lot of support. Select newer varieties that are sturdier or more compact and which require little or no staking.

• Those perennials that do need some support will look more natural if you use twigs rather than canes or metal hoops to support them. Do not be afraid to allow some perennials to 'flop-about' since they contribute to the natural look of the garden.

• Grow climbers up walls, fences and up shrubs and trees. The only thing better than the old gnarled leaning apple tree is an old gnarled leaning apple tree with a rose or clematis growing up it.

• Allow plants to self-seed in borders and amongst paving and don't be afraid of using some species repetitively throughout the garden to help create that vital feeling of unity.

PLANTS DIRECTORY

The following plants all have a cottage garden 'feel' about them and will help you to create a cottage garden style. Many are perennials that form the basis of all good examples of such gardens.

Plants are listed in alphabetical order of Latin name followed by the common name, if any. The common name is excluded if it is identical to the Latin name.

The 'fact line' shows, in order:
Size – average height in metres and spread in metres of a mature plant
Soil – tolerances, preferences or special requirements
Site – tolerances, preferences or special requirements

ACHILLEA YARROW

An important genus of herbaceous perennials, most with large flat 'plates' of minute daisy-like flowers produced all summer, excellent for cutting and drying, and feather-like foliage.

A. 'Coronation Gold' – a tall variety with bright yellow flowers.

A. 'Moonshine' – soft, sulphur yellow flowers and greyish foliage.

A. ptarmica 'Boule de Neige' (syn. *A. p.* 'The Pearl') – pure white, double flowers on branching heads.

0.5 to 1.0 × 0.5   Well-drained loam   Sun or shade

ACONITUM MONKSHOOD

Beautiful summer or late summer and early autumn flowering perennials with poisonous roots (so don't plant them where they may be dug up and mistaken for a vegetable). The common name describes the hooded flower shape.

A. 'Bressingham Spire' – violet-blue flowers on sturdy stems.

A. carmichaelii – a wonderful tall species with the best deeply divided lush green foliage of the group and light blue flowers.

0.9 to 1.5 × 0.5   Well-drained loam   Sun or shade

ALCEA HOLLYHOCK

Hollyhocks are a classic cottage garden plant. Although perennial, they tend to be short-lived and many gardeners grow them from seed on a regular basis.

A. ficifolia – good clean foliage and huge spikes of single yellow flowers.

A. rosea – the typical species, normally seen in various forms such as Chater's Double (mixed colours) or 'Nigra' which has extraordinary Chocolate-maroon flowers. Double forms are normally found under the heading 'Powder-Puff' and are red, pink, white or yellow.

1.2 to 3.0 × 0.8   Well-drained   Sun

ALCHEMILLA MOLLIS LADY'S MANTLE

A good 'indicator' plant for any would-be cottage gardener.

Achillea

Alchemilla mollis

Anchusa azurea 'Loddon Royalist'

Alcea rosea

Antirrhinum

Loose sprays of tiny yellow-green flowers appear in early summer above broad downy leaves that are able to catch and hold rain and dew drops. If you do not cut the flower heads off it will seed itself around delightfully but profusely.

0.5 × 0.5   Any fertile soil   Sun or shade

ANCHUSA
Old fashioned-looking perennials with rich blue borage-like flowers in early summer. 'Loddon Royalist' is a fine popular form and 'Little John' is a good dwarf (0.5 m).

0.5 to 1.0 × 0.6   Well-drained   Sun

ANEMONE × HYBRIDA JAPANESE ANEMONE
These are tough, and somewhat invasive perennials that produce a magnificent display of daisy-like flowers in late summer and early autumn. Although tall they do not need staking. The original plant has pink flowers with a yellow centre. 'Honorine Jobert' is probably the best white variety. Also look out for 'Queen Charlotte' (pink) and *A. hupehensis* var. *japonica* 'Bressingham Glow' (semi-double, rose-red).

1.2 × 0.6   Any soil   Sun or shade

ANTIRRHINUM SNAPDRAGON
A tender short-lived perennial normally grown as a bedding plant. The tubular flowers or 'bunny rabbits' are among the first to be noticed by children. Available in a wide range of mixed-colour varieties that are tall, medium or dwarf, but perhaps the most restrained colour forms, such as 'Yellow Monarch' or 'Purple King' (lilac/purple), are best for the cottage garden .

0.3 to 0.45 × 0.3   Light soil   Sun

AQUILEGIA COLUMBINE
A large group of much-loved, dainty perennials with distinct winged and spurred flowers. *A. vulgaris* is the common Euro-

Aquilegia

pean species (granny's bonnets) which has red, violet, pink or white flowers in early summer. The McKana and Monarch hybrids are useful mixed colour strains. 'Nora Barlow' is a charming double. All seed themselves around and are a must for the cottage garden.

0.6 to 0.4   Well-drained soil   Cool sun or part shade

ARMERIA THRIFT OR SEA PINK
Useful edging perennial with grass-like leaves in hummocks and globular heads of tiny flowers from May to July.
A. maritima – a coastal native with pink flowers, but there are various cultivated forms such as 'Alba' (white flowers) and 'Vindictive' (a good red).
A. allicacea (syn. *A. plantaginea*) – a taller species with broader leaves and larger flower heads.

0.2 to 0.4 × 0.3   Well-drained, especially chalk   Sun

ARTEMISIA
Aromatic silver or grey-leaved perennials grown for their foliage, except *A. lactiflora* (1.5 × 0.6 m) which has beautiful

creamy-white flowers on erect stems in late summer. *A. abrotanum* is the herb southernwood with feathery sage-green leaves. *A. absinthium* is wormwood which has deeply-cut silver foliage. The best dwarf is *A.* 'Canescens'. *A. ludoviciana* and its varieties have stunning grey-white willow-like leaves, sometimes with jagged edges and running roots.

0.5 to 0.9 × 0.6   Well-drained   Sun

ASTER MICHAELMAS DAISY

Another typical perennial of cottage gardens. The true Michaelmas daisy and most common is *A. novi-belgii* which has hundreds of named varieties, many of which are prone to pest and disease or have an 'over-bred', unbalanced look about them. Other, lesser-known species are worth trying. *A. amellus* is a stocky, self-supporter with violet and pink flower forms. *A.* × *frikartii* is perhaps the best aster of all, having good, clean foliage, strong stems and the most wonderful sky-blue flowers with yellow stamens from July to October. There are several small-flowered species that flower in autumn and early winter that are ideal for the cottage garden, including *A. ericoides, A. cordifolius* and *A. pilosus* var. *demotus*.

0.6 to 1.3 × 0.4   Any soil   Sun or part shade

Armeria maritima

Aster × frikartii

Bellis perennis

BELLIS PERENNIS DAISY

This hardy perennial, today usually considered only as a lawn weed, was cherished by the cottage gardeners of old who used them as edgers or in containers. There are a number of forms, many of them very old in origin. 'Dresden China' has dusky pink button-like flowers which seem to be present all-year-round. 'Rob Roy' is similar but red and 'Prolifera', the hen and chickens daisy, has small flowerlets which develop from a larger central bloom mimicking chicks around the mother hen. These are humble little plants, but nonetheless charming.

0.15 × 0.2   Any soil   Sun or part shade

BUDDLEJA BUTTERFLY OR BOMBSITE BUSH

These deciduous shrubs so beloved by bees and butterflies, bear honey-scented flower spikes in mid-summer. *B. davidii* and its many varieties is the most common, but for the cottage garden *B. alternifolia* with its arching stems of lilac flowers makes an unusual alternative.

3.0 × 2.5   Any well-drained soil   Any site

CAMPANULA BELL-FLOWER

Perennials that are anything from compact edgers to tall billowing clumps for the mixed border. They include some of the best plants for the cottage garden and have a long tradition: *C. persicifolia* was introduced in Tudor times. The blue flowers readily seed themselves around as does the white form. 'Pride of Exmouth' and 'Fleur de Neige' are doubles. *C. trachelium* has nettle-like leaves and purple-blue flowers, but look out for 'Bernice', a fine variety with double flowers. The dwarfs include *C. carpatica* and the dainty fairy thimbles, *C. cochleariifolia*. These will spread amongst paving or up into old walls. *C. medium* is the ancient hardy biennial Canterbury bell with white, mauve and blue cup and saucer type flowers. All are summer flowering.

0.1 to 1.2 × 0.2 to 0.5   Well-drained soil   Sun or part shade

CENTAUREA KNAPWEED OR CORNFLOWER

C. montana is the perennial mountain knapweed grown for centuries in gardens. The blue, white or pink flowers appear in June. *C. hypoleuca* 'John Coutts' is an especially good variety with deep rose flowers in early summer and again in autumn. *C. macrocephala* has rich yellow flowers that dry well. *C. cyanus* is the hardy annual with pink, red, blue or white flowers that are excellent for cutting or drying.

0.8 × 0.5   Well-drained, especially chalk   Sun or part shade

CLEMATIS

A very important genus of woody-climbers. Many of the large-flowered hybrids, although excellent garden plants, are perhaps too 'loud' for the cottage garden style. Many of the species and their hybrids however are definitely worthy of inclusion.

C. flammula – in Britain since the 16th century. Masses of small creamy-white flowers with the scent of meadowsweet are produced in autumn.

C. alpina – with blue, white or rose-red flower forms appear-

Campanula medium

Clematis macropetala

Clematis viticella 'Abundance'

ing in April and May is less vigorous and ideal for growing amongst deciduous shrubs.

C. viticella – a small-flowered species cultivated for hundreds of years. There are some excellent named varieties and hybrids such as 'Alba Luxurians' (white), 'Royal Velours' (deep purple) and 'Purpurea Plena Elegans' (lilac-purple, double).

2.0 to 5.0 × 1.5 to 4.0   Cool, moist but well-drained
Sun or part shade

CONVALLARIA MAJALIS LILY OF THE VALLEY

These plants are miniature delights with their broad lance-shaped leaves and small arching stems of pendant white bells appearing together in April to May. Plant in a shady position near the house to enjoy the spicy night scent. Cut for the house – and, traditionally, for bridal bouquets. It is a perennial that spreads by underground rhizomes.

0.15 × 0.15   Moist soil   Full or part shade

CORYLUS COMMON HAZEL

A native deciduous shrub suitable for hedging or left to form a small tree. The yellow catkin flowers appear in February before the leaves unfurl. *C. maxima* is the filbert, long-cultivated for its nuts and parent of numerous named varieties, 'Kentish Cob' being the most widely available. These are charming, utilitarian cottage garden shrubs.

2.0 to 5.0 × 3.0   Any soil   Any site

CYNARA SCOLYMUS GLOBE ARTICHOKE

A giant, dual-purpose perennial and a truly ornamental vegetable. The superb grey and divided leaves provide a strong contrast to smaller foliage. The violet, thistle-like flower heads are also the gastronome's delight. The cardoon (*C. cardunculus*) is a prickly relative of equal stature with young leaves that are delicious when blanched.

1.8 × 0.9   Well-drained   Full sun

DAHLIA

This famous group of tender perennials with tuberous roots was the most fashionable flower in the country in the early to mid 19th century. At that time there were well over 800 named varieties. There are many different flower types and colours, although some are a little brassy and garish for the true cottage garden. The Singles, Collerettes, Peony flowered and Pompon types, however, have a rightful place in any

Convallaria majalis

Cynara scolymus

Dahlia

Daphne odora 'Aureomarginata'

Delphinium

Dianthus barbatus

Dianthus 'Lilian'

cottage garden. Grow amongst plants that will give winter cover and you may get away with not lifting and storing the tubers every autumn.

0.4 to 1.5 × 0.3 to 0.6   Moist soils except waterlogged
Sun or part shade

....

DAPHNE

Evergreen and deciduous shrubs of special merit for any style of garden. A couple of species are especially appropriate for the cottage garden.

D. mezereum – the fragrant, native mezereon. The purple-red flowers are produced in early spring. It has been cultivated since the 16th century.

D. odora is an evergreen from China and Japan with purple and white flowers in winter and early spring that have a strong, sweet scent that is detectable from some distance away. In a vase they will scent a room for many days.

0.5 to 1.5 × 0.5 to 2.0   Well-drained but moisture retentive
Sheltered sun or part shade

....

DELPHINIUM

This group of mainly tall-growing annual and perennial flowers has a strong association with cottage gardens. Choose your flower colours carefully – many are very insistent and too 'modern'-looking for a cottage garden. Although there are a number of species, it is the garden hybrids that are the most readily available, especially the Astolat, Black Knight, Blue Fountains, Galahad, New Century and Pacific Hybrid groups. Also seek out the more delicate Belladonna hybrids.

0.6 to 2.0 × 0.4 to 0.9   Well-drained   Sun

....

DIANTHUS CARNATION, PINK OR SWEET WILLIAM

Perhaps the most important of all summer flowering cottage garden perennials. Some go back to Chaucer's time and although many are now lost the number of varieties available is still great. The main types suitable for the cottage garden are:

D. barbatus – sweet William; a perennial but usually treated as a biennial.

D. caryophyllus – carnations; these include the delightful clove carnations which carry a rich clove perfume, for example 'Lord Chatham' and 'Fenbow Nutmeg Clove'.

D. plumarius – pinks; this is the largest group with new varieties selected out every century since the 14th, such as 'Sops-in-Wine' (14th century), 'Caesar's Mantle' (16th), 'Painted Lady' (17th), 'Musgrave's Pink' (syn. 'Green Eyes') (c.1730), 'Chelsea Pink' (18th), 'Mrs Sinkins' (19th) and 'Freckles' (20th). All have blue/grey foliage with delicate and highly scented flowers. There are also some very important strains such as the laced pinks and the Allwoodii Group. There are a number of nurseries that specialize in these beautiful plants and further information can be obtained from the various books devoted to them. Although quite short-lived, all are easily propagated from heeled cuttings, torn off and placed in the open ground in September. Some of the modern varieties, it has to be said, flower more prolifically than the older varieties, among them 'Doris' (pink and red), 'Laced Monarch' (pink and chestnut), 'Haytor' (white) and 'Gran's Favourite' (white and red).

0.3 × 0.3   Well-drained soil   Sun

DIGITALIS FOXGLOVE

Digitalis purpurea is a native biennial which will seed itself around. There are good pale pink and white forms. *D. grandiflora* is shorter but a perennial with delightful soft-yellow flowers.

0.6 to 1.2 × 0.3   Any soil   Sun or shade

ERYSIMUM WALLFLOWER

The common bedder *E. cheiri,* formerly *Cheiranthus,* is actually a perennial with highly fragrant, spring flowers in most colours except white and blue. 'Harpur Crewe' is a double. *E. allionii* is the dwarf yellow or orange Siberian Wallflower.

Erysimum

The perennial wallflowers, are short-lived (but easily re-prop-agated from cuttings) woody plants well worth including in any cottage garden. There are some splendid colour forms, mainly yellow or purple that are seldom out of flower. 'Bowles' Mauve' is widely available, but others such as 'Bredon' (yellow) and 'Constant Cheer' (orange-brown) are worth sourcing.

0.45 × 0.3   Any soil including poor and dry   Sun

GALANTHUS NIVALIS SNOWDROP

A bulbous perennial with unmistakable small, white nodding flowers from January to March that are slightly fragrant. They like a cool shady position and give early colour to the cottage garden.

0.2 × 0.2   Moist but well-drained soil   Light shade

GERANIUM CRANE'S-BILL

A genus of mostly perennial plants that includes several British natives. They are easy to grow and invaluable in a

Geranium pratense 'Mrs Kendall Clark'

Geranium sanguineum

cottage garden. Many are good ground-coverers and all produce long-lasting, beautiful flowers and have attractive, often deeply divided leaves.

G. pratense – the native meadow crane's-bill is a very handsome plant with violet-blue flowers. There are some even better double forms of it.

G. sanguineum – the bloody crane's-bill is another good cottage garden plant with magenta flowers. There are white and light pink forms.

These two species in particular have long been grown in cottage gardens so are first choice for the purist but the other crane's-bills should not be dismissed.

0.2 to 1.0 X 0.4 to 1.0   Any soil except boggy   Sun or shade

GEUM AVENS OR HERB BENNET

G. urbanum is a dainty native perennial with pale yellow flowers. Long grown in cottage gardens, it has a number of medicinal uses. Nicolas Culpepper, the famous herbalist, suggested that 'its warm savour was useful to expel crude humours from the belly'. The pleasantly aromatic roots were once used as a substitute for cloves and to flavour ale. In the modern cottage garden perhaps *G. chiloense* has a place, particularly 'Lady Stratheden' (double, warm yellow) and 'Mrs J. Bradshaw'

Geum chiloense 'Lady Stratheden'

25

Gypsophilia 'Rosy Veil'

(brick red). For cooler, wetter soils *G. rivale* is ideal. The flowers are bell-shaped and a warm coppery pink.

0.3 × 0.2   Well-drained   Sun or light shade

....

GYPSOPHILA BABY'S BREATH

Although they are not historically associated with cottage gardens, the billowy clouds of small, mainly white flowers from June to August make a wonderful contrast to larger flowers in the cottage garden border. Plant with oriental poppies to hide their browning leaves after flowering.

G. paniculata – the common species and 'Bristol Fairy', which has pure white, double flowers is one of the best varieties.

G. 'Rosy Veil' – a compact hybrid with pink, double blooms.

0.2 to 1.2 × 0.4 to 1.2   Deep, well-drained, preferably non-acid
Sun or light shade

....

HEDERA IVY

European woody climbers that will attach themselves by aerial roots to walls or tree trunks or will spread along the ground as

Hedera helix

Helianthus annus

a carpet. *H. helix*, the British native, has provided us with many attractive forms. The smaller-leaved types are especially appropriate for a cottage garden and include 'Caenwoodiana' (divided, narrow lobed leaves), 'Glacier' (silver-grey leaves with a white edge) and 'Parsley Crested' (pale green, wavy and crinkled leaves).

3.0 to 6.0 × 2.0 to 3.0   Any soil   Sun or shade

HELIANTHUS ANNUS SUNFLOWER

A hardy annual, loved by children, with yellow daisy flowers the size of plates that follow the sun. They have been grown in cottage gardens since the 16th century. Today there are many interesting forms available from the seedsman. 'Sunspot' grows to only 0.6 m. 'Velvet Queen' has chocolate-coloured flowers. There are also strains of mixed colours available. There is something strangely humorous about sunflowers and they are always fun to see.

0.6 to 3.0 × 0.4   Well-drained   Sun

HELIOTROPIUM HELIOTROPE OR CHERRY PIE

Cherry pie (*H. peruvianum*) was a common cottage garden flower in Victorian times, but, sadly, it is seldom seen today. Although a perennial, it is tender and is usually treated as a bedding annual. It can, however, be over-wintered in pots in the home where it may flower again. The dark purple flowers are tiny but appear in large bunches. The common name describes the scent – just like ripe cherries baked in a pie. There are white and blue flowered forms too.

0.45 × 0.30   Well-drained   Sun

HELLEBORUS CHRISTMAS AND LENTEN ROSES

Summer tends to be the main season of display in a cottage garden, so these evergreen, winter and early spring flowering perennials can provide vital structure and interest at a time when a border would otherwise look drab and empty.

H. niger – the Christmas rose has white flowers. The black roots used to be dried and taken as snuff to cure headaches and melancholia.

H. foetidus – has beautiful finger-like dark green leaves and green flowers.

H. argutifolius – has similar coloured flowers atop grey-green serrated leaves.

0.3 to 0.6 × 0.4 to 0.9   Moist but well-drained   Partial shade

HEMEROCALLIS DAYLILY

Easily grown, summer flowering perennials with each funnel-shaped bloom lasting only a day, although the overall display persists for a good two months. They have been grown for hundreds of years, the early varieties being various shades of orange or yellow. Today the colour range is much larger and includes reds, maroons and pinks. The flower petals are very tasty and can be used in salads.

0.8 × 0.6   Any soil   Sun or light shade

Heliotropium

Helleborus argutifolius

Hemerocallis 'Prima Donna'

Iris sibirica 'Heavenly Blue'

HUMULUS LUPULUS HOP

A native perennial climber grown for many hundreds of years for flavouring beer. Herbalists attributed many medicinal uses. Culpepper recommended it for 'opening obstructions of the liver and spleen, cleansing the blood, loosening the belly, expelling the gravel and provoking the urine'. The flowers are supposed to be a mild sedative – hence hop pillows – and are attractive when dried. It is normally seen as the yellow–leaved variety 'Aureus' which, sadly, is shy of flowering. It is a fine climber for the porch or covered gateway.

3.0 to 6.0 × 3.0   Any soil   Sun or shade

IRIS

A very large group of hardy perennials with either rhizoma-tous or bulbous roots. Some are large flowering tall plants but at the other extreme they can be miniature alpines suitable for a small pot. Perhaps the largest and most popular group are the bearded irises that originate from *I. germanica*. They flower in June and the colour range is massive. Others to consider for the cottage garden include:

I. sibirica – grown in Elizabethan gardens, it has elegant grass-like foliage and mainly blue flowers.

I. unguicularis – the winter-flowering iris for poor, dry soils.

0.10 to 1.2 × 0.2 to 0.4   As a group, almost any soil is tolerated
Sun or part shade

JASMINUM JASMINE

Woody climbers grown for their flowers, which in some species are powerfully scented. The winter jasmine, *J. nudiflorum*, which is not scented, was brought from China in 1844, and its yellow flowers in December and January were soon appreciated. It may be trained on to trellis or a wall. The common white jasmine (*J. officinale*) was grown in cottage gardens as far back as the mid 16th century. The deliciously fragrant flowers appear from June to September. The form *affine* is superior.

3.0 × 2.0   Fertile soil   Sun

LATHYRUS PERENNIAL PEA

These perennial climbers are essential plants for a cottage garden. They can be seen trained up bean sticks or allowed to

Lathyrus grandiflorus

Lavandula stoechas subsp. *pendunculata*

Lavatera 'Rosea'

ramble over shrubs and in hedges or to sprawl along the ground.

L. grandiflorus – humorously called the everlasting pea, has rose and pink flowers from June to September.

L. latifolius – the true perennial pea is the most associated with cottage gardens in which it has grown since the early 17th century. The flowers are magenta-pink but there is a good white form.

L. odoratus – the scented annual sweet pea also has a long cottage garden history. In more recent years it has become a much-loved 'hobby plant' for exhibition purposes. There are many named varieties to choose from, some with highly-bred garish flower colours. For the cottage garden choose wisely and try to source those that still have a good scent, such as 'Cream Beauty', 'Painted Lady' and 'Leamington'.

2.0 × 1.0   Moist but well-drained   Sun or part shade

LAVANDULA LAVENDER

Much-prized aromatic woody sub-shrubs, the grey-green leaves are full of essential oils that have been put to a wide range of uses since the 16th century. Dried, the flowers were placed between stored linen or under pillows to encourage sleep. The term 'hot lavender' refers to its use as a comforter and drier of head colds. Lavender has maintained its popularity better than any other cottage garden plant. The profuse blue flowers and soft foliage combine well with most other plants. It makes an excellent low hedge or 'full stop' plant, especially good with ruby coloured roses or old fashioned pinks – and much loved by bees. The various pink and white forms of lavender are generally disappointing, being inferior in both flower colour and quantity to the blues.

L. angustifolia – common lavender, which includes the dwarfer, darker forms 'Munstead' and 'Hidcote'.

L. stoechas – French lavender; purple flowers with attractive, long bracts.

0.3 to 0.9 × 0.3 to 0.5   Well-drained   Full sun

LAVATERA TREE MALLOW

This vigorous woody shrub is a good example of a 'modern' plant that has a cottage garden feel about it. *L. olbia* has large pink or reddish-pink mallow flowers all through summer and a loose, 'blousy' habit. The various hybrids are more usually seen, 'Rosea', with pink flowers, being the oldest. More recently, 'Barnsley' has been introduced with pale pink flowers that have a red eye (sadly liable to revert), a good white ('Ice Cool') and a purple pink ('Burgundy Wine').

2.0 × 2.0   Any well-drained soil   Warm and full sun

LILIUM LILY

These bulbous perennials must have been amongst the most prized possessions of the cottage gardeners of old. They have quite specific cultural requirements which vary from species to species. More than anything else most require good drainage. Plant the bulbs deep (20 cm) with plenty of coarse grit underneath, except for Madonna lilies which should be planted just beneath the soil surface. During this century, many hybrids and varieties have been bred which are less fussy about growing conditions but eminently suitable for the cottage garden. Scented types are especially appropriate. Here is a selection of the best:

L. candidum – Madonna lily, pure white, fragrant; prefers chalk.

L. lancifolium (syn. *L. tigrinum*) – tiger lily, deep orange with black spots; humus rich soil.

L. martagon – Turk's cap lily, soft pink, recurving petals.

L. pardalinum – leopard lily, yellow or orange; tolerates wet clay and shade.

0.6 to 1.5 × 0.3   Almost any soil type tolerated   Sun or shade

LONICERA PERICLYMENUM HONEYSUCKLE OR WOODBINE
Our common native honeysuckle that originally must have been part of the cottage hedgerow or was dug up and planted in the garden to scramble over arbours or around the front door. The fragrance of the purplish and yellow trumpet flowers is especially pronounced in the evening when it is visited

by hawk-moths. The variety 'Belgica' flowers earlier (May and June) and 'Serotina' later (July to October). Do not be afraid of trying other climbing honeysuckles such as:

L. sempervirens 'Dropmore Scarlet' – scarlet flowers from July to October.

L. × heckrottii 'Gold Flame' – bright yellow flushed purple flowers from July to September.

L. japonica 'Halliana' – almost evergreen with powerfully fragrant yellow and cream flowers from June to September.

Lonicera periclymenum
'Serotina'

4.0 × 2.0   Fertile loam   Sun or part shade

Lilium candium

LUNARIA ANNUA HONESTY

A pleasing biennial both in flower (purple or white) and when in seed (a spray of flat silvery moons, hence the Latin name). It has been grown in Britain since at least Tudor times when it was considered that it grew well only in the gardens of honest people. The roots, boiled and grated into soups or on meat, was thought to ensure good health. Honesty readily seeds itself around, popping up in a different place every year. The flowers appear in April. The seed is extensively used in flower arranging. Look out for *L. rediviva*, a lilac-white flowered perennial version.

0.9 × 0.4   Well-drained   Sun or shade

LUPINUS LUPIN

A common easy to grow perennial with fat, erect spikes of pea flowers. *L. polyphyllus,* the main species, with blue flowers in early summer, has given rise to many coloured forms including the Russell Hybrids introduced by George Russell of York in the 1930s. More recent varieties worth trying include 'My Castle' (red) and 'Noble Maiden' (white and ivory). *L. arboreus*, the tree lupin, is really a shrub reaching 1.5 m high and across. Fragrant, clear yellow flowers are produced in August.

1.0 × 0.6   Well-drained – not chalk   Sun

LYCHNIS CHALCEDONICA JERUSALEM CROSS

The common name of this perennial describes the cross formed by the red flower petals in early summer. It was introduced during the Crusades and is easy to grow in any soil type.

0.9 × 1.2   Any soil   Sun

MATTHIOLA STOCK

A wonderful group of highly-scented annual or biennial flowers. There are four main groups, the first three developed from *M. incana*:

Ten week stock – the double flowers appear ten weeks after

Lunaria annua

Matthiola incana

Lupinus (Russell Hybrids)

sowing in summer and are various shades of pink, blue and yellow. The Excelsior Mammoth strain is especially good.

Brompton stock – sown in summer for flowering the following spring. Mixtures are available of white, purple, crimson and rose.

East Lothian stock – flowers in autumn until the first frosts.

Night-scented stock (*M. longipetala* subsp. *bicornis*) – can be sown in April where you want it to flower. The lilac or purple flowers fill the garden with a rich perfume on warm summer evenings.

0.3 to 0.45 × 0.3   Well-drained limy soil preferred
Sun or light shade

MENTHA MINT

Most herbs look at home in a cottage garden, and the mint tribe is no exception to this. The aromatic leaves have many uses, especially, of course, in the kitchen. They tend to be invasive so plant in some form of container and then sink into the ground. There are many species and forms, some highly decorative:

M. suaveolens – apple mint; large round hairy leaves, one of the best for cooking.

M. × *villosa* nm. *alopecuroides* – Bowles' mint; fine fresh flavour – the connoisseur's mint.

M. × *piperata* nm. *citrata* – eau de Cologne mint; very sweet for teas, vinegars and fruit drinks or in pot pourris.

0.6 × 0.6   Any well-drained soil   Sun or part shade

MESPILUS GERMANICA MEDLAR

This is a small deciduous tree with a delightfully crooked and picturesque habit that makes specimens look much older than they actually are. The wild medlar is not a native but has naturalized in several southern counties. It has long been cultivated for its fruit which are like small brown apples and an acquired taste. They have to be allowed to rot (bletted) before consumption. This is a beautiful tree both in leaf (long

Mentha suaveolens 'Variegata'   *Monarda didyma*

and downy) and in flower (single, white, quite large in late May and early June), and almost invites one to sit beneath it.

5.0 × 4.0   Any soil except boggy   Sun or part shade

MONARDA DIDYMA BERGAMOT OR BEE BALM

A pretty herb for the cottage garden border, with aromatic leaves, stems and roots that give off a lemon scent when crushed. It is used in perfumery and in pot pourris and the infused leaves make Oswego tea. The unusual hooded red, pink, purple or white flowers appear from July to September. Good hybrids include 'Croftway Pink' (rose-pink) and 'Prairie Night' (purple).

0.9 × 0.5   Moist soil but tolerates dry   Sun or light shade

MORUS MULBERRY

This small deciduous tree has a rugged old-world charm that is very much in keeping with the cottage garden style. The

Nepeta × faassenii (foreground)

large often lobed leaves have a bold texture and the fruits of course are delicious if you manage to get them before the birds. *M. alba* (white mulberry) and *M. nigra* (black mulberry) are the two species normally grown. Both were introduced in the 16th century.

5.0 × 5.0   Well-drained   Sun

NEPETA CATMINT

These perennials make good edging or ground-covering plants. Their subdued greyish foliage and principally blue flowers soften and combine well with most other colours. Flowering is long, May to September. Cats love to roll over and chew the aromatic leaves.

N. × *faassenii* – the commonest catmint.
N. 'Six Hills Giant' – larger in every part.

0.4 to 0.9 × 0.8   Well-drained soils including poor   Sun

NIGELLA LOVE-IN-A-MIST

The common name of this hardy annual describes the misty blue flowers that nestle amongst the filigree foliage. Its been around since Elizabethan times and in those earlier days the black seeds were used to flavour cakes or warmed over hot ashes to scent a musty room. Crushed into powder and mixed with vinegar, it was claimed that the seed 'taketh away freckles'. *N. damascena* is the usual species grown. Just sow the seeds in autumn or early spring where they are to flower. There are good named forms. The dried seed-heads are used in flower arranging.

0.4 × 0.3   Well-drained   Sun or light shade

OENOTHERA EVENING PRIMROSE

O. biennis (syn. *O. glabra*) is the biennial species of old cottage gardens that was introduced in the early 17th century. For today's cottage garden perhaps some of the perennial evening primroses are equally appropriate. The best is surely *O. macrocarpa* (syn. *O. missouriensis*), a low, prostrate plant with huge yellow flowers from July to September. *O. fruticosa* subsp. *glauca* (syn. *O. tetragona*) is upright with inferior flowers but fine red flushed foliage in spring. The common name refers to the fact that the flowers open fully only at that time of day.

0.2 to 0.5 × 0.5   Prefers light well-drained soil   Sun

Nigella damascena

Oenothera fruticosa subsp. *glauca*

PAEONIA PEONY

These long-lived aristocratic perennials are the quitessential cottage garden plants. To create such a garden without their inclusion would be unthinkable. The attractive, often richly-bronzed foliage in spring is quickly followed in May by fragrant flowers of supreme quality. In autumn the foliage is tinted again and the opening pods reveal brightly coloured seeds. *P. officinalis*, the common peony, is an old favourite with white or red double flowered forms. The most popular group today is the Chinese or June-flowering peony (*P. lactiflora*) which is the parent of a large, highly-bred group of hybrids and many named forms. There are a number of different flower shapes, including double, semi-double and anemone. Other species are also available, 'Mollie-the-witch' (*P. mlokosewitschii*), for example, which flowers very early (April to May) and deserves a special prominent position where its cool yellow, scented flowers can be fully appreciated.

0.6 × 0.6   Any fertile soil   Sun or a little shade

PAPAVER ORIENTALE ORIENTAL POPPY

A popular perennial with large bowl-shaped flowers surrounding a dark boss of anthers. Varieties range in colour from white, through orange to deep red. Some of the best are 'Goliath' (tall stems, deep red flowers), 'Cedric Morris' (misty pink) and 'Perry's White' (white). After flowering from May to June, the foliage can look tatty so always plant them where later flowers will hide them. *P. somniferum* is the showy annual opium poppy that will seed itself around. *P. rhoeas* is our native red-flowered corn poppy, also an annual

0.9 × 0.4   Well-drained   Sun

PHILADELPHUS MOCK ORANGE

Small, medium or large deciduous shrubs, often called syringa (which is the Latin name of lilac). *P. coronarius* was possibly the first species introduced (by the Romans) from central Italy.

Paeonia lactiflora 'Sarah Bernhardt'

Paeonia officinalis 'Rubra Plena'

Philadelphus 'Belle Etoile'

Papaver orientale

Most of the mock oranges available today are hybrids but virtually all are at home in the cottage garden. Some of the best are:

'Beauclerk' – medium sized, with single white flowers.

'Belle Etoile' – compact with fragrant single white blooms flushed maroon in the centre.

'Virginal' – vigorous and large, white double flowers with a rich perfume.

P. microphyllus – a delightful little species with dainty leaves and fragrant white flowers.

1.0 to 4.0 × 1.0 to 3.0   Any soil   Sun or part shade

PRIMULA AURICULA BEAR'S EARS OR BORDER AURICULA
Many members of the Primula family are associated with cottage gardens, but none more so than the auricula. These are plants of great antiquity (thought to have been introduced into Britain in the late 16th century), rich flower colour and tough constitution. The powerful scent from April to June is especially pronounced on hot days. Their large clusters of variously coloured blooms amid fleshy, almost succulent, leaves give a fine show in a pot or along a path edge. A few old forms can be found such as 'Old Red Dusty Miller', which like many varieties is covered by a light bloom

Rosa 'Fantin-Latour'

44

giving the impression that the whole plant has been sprinkled with flour. The flowers are crimson-brown and highly scented. These should not be confused with the amazing but delicate Show and Alpine auriculas which are just as old but are grown under glass by many enthusiasts for exhibition purposes.

Sadly there is not enough room to cover the genus properly in these pages but one should at least mention the pure and simple cowslip (*P. veris*) and primrose (*P. vulgaris*), the latter being parent to some ancient and beautiful strains such as the Jack-in-the-Greens (ruffled flowers), hose-in-hose (cup and saucer petals) types and the many doubles, especially those bred by the famous Barnhaven nursery.

0.15 × 0.15   Deep, rich, moist but well-drained   Sun or
light shade

ROSA ROSE
One could write a book just about roses for cottage gardens, and all that can be dealt with here are some basic suggestions.

Hybrid Tea (Large-flowered) and Floribunda (Cluster roses) are the more recent descendants of what are generally termed the old-fashioned or shrub roses. Although some modern varieties of roses fit the cottage garden picture, the most appropriate first choices would be from amongst the older groups. The term 'old fashioned' actually covers a number of different groups of shrubs, climbers and rambler roses, some of them quite new, as well as the many wild species. Do not assume that all old roses are too big, too thorny, disease-ridden and with only pink or white in flowers that only lasts a few days: nothing could be further from the truth, and every group contains varieties that more than dispel these myths. Some of the old roses are actually miniature in size, and a few are actually thorn*less*. Yes, it is true that some of the wild roses will get very big, but in a cottage garden (or any type of garden) this can be very useful – for example as a flowering screen, windbreak or hedge.

Apart from these, every group of old and shrub roses contains varieties that could be fitted comfortably into a 1.0 m × 1.0 m space. Careful selection will avoid those prone to disease. The Alba and Rugosa roses are particularly strong on this. Having said that, diseases on old roses never seem to look as bad as they do on the modern types.

The flowers of old and species roses could not be more diverse. Every colour is represented except the blues, and they can be small delicate single flowers or huge many-petalled doubles such as those of the Cabbage or Centifolia roses. Their colour is more refined and subtle when compared with some of the highly bred modern varieties. They often fade or deepen in colour as they go over, giving a wonderful tonal quality to the petals.

Because of the various myths about old roses there was a period in the middle of this century when, for the first time, they became unfashionable. As a result many varieties have been lost. Fortunately they are now very much appreciated and thanks to two nurserymen in particular, Peter Beales and David Austin, a large number are readily available.

Lack of space prevents mentioning all the many hundreds of varieties that are suitable – but here is a shortlist of some of the best (see the Checklists for more):

R. gallica var. officinalis – the apothecary's rose; light crimson double flowers in June. Introduced to Europe by returning crusaders in the 13th century, originally to the French town of Provins, where it was and is the basis of an industry that exploited its chemical and medicinal properties.

R. gallica 'Versicolor' – another Gallica rose with crimson double flowers, spotted, striped and speckled with pale pink; named Rosa Mundi after Fair Rosamund, the mistress of Henry II.

R. 'Maiden's Blush' – an Alba rose with fresh blush-pink double flowers that are richly scented (pre-15th century).

R. × centifolia – the original rose of the Centifolia or Cabbage group. Large bright pink fully double flowers and very highly

Rosa gallica

Rosa 'Cécile Brunner'

scented; immortalized on the canvases of Dutch and Flemish still life painters (pre-1600).

R. 'Mme Isaac Pereire' – a Bourbon rose, possibly the most powerfully fragrant of all roses. Huge, purple-crimson flowers bulging with petals. Quite large, but if you've only got room for one rose in your garden this is the one.

R. 'Cornelia' – one of the many brilliant Hybrid Musk roses that have a very long flowering period and make tough sturdy bushes. The salmon-pink buds open to an unusual apricot pink flushed with strawberry pink. Very fragrant.

R. 'Cécile Brunner' - the sweetheart rose, only a metre high, with small shapely flowers, highly scented and a soft delicate pink. There is a famous climbing form too.

R. 'White Pet' – a species form that gets no taller than 0.6 m. The densely-petalled blooms are creamy-white and appear from June to the first frosts.

R. 'Graham Thomas' – the group of English roses bred by David Austin over the last 30 years combines the best of old and new roses: good fragrance, foliage, disease resistance and long flowering. 'Graham Thomas', a good example of the group, has rich yellow flowers and a Tea rose scent.

Any self-respecting cottage garden must include climbing roses. Here are a few to whet your appetite:

R. 'Climbing Etoile de Hollande' – not that old (1931). Large rich velvety crimson flowers with a powerful scent.

R. 'Climbing Pompon de Paris' – pretty button-like flowers and fern-like foliage. Useful where space is at a premium.

R. 'Rambling Rector' – probably c.1900; an old rambler with clusters of double white flowers and a delicious fragrance followed by good hips in the autumn.

R. 'Zéphirine Drouhin' – a Bourbon climber, thornless, with semi-double cerise-pink flowers that are very sweetly scented.

0.4 to 3.0 × 0.5 to 3.0   Most well-drained soils   Sun or light shade

ROSMARINUS OFFICINALIS ROSEMARY

An evergreen aromatic shrub introduced into Britain in the

Salvia officinalis

14th century. The greyish-green narrow leaves make an excellent foil to the clusters of blue flowers in April and May. Rosemary, as well as being attractive, has many uses. Oil of rosemary is an ingredient of perfume and the fresh foliage under a pillow encourages a peaceful sleep. It was also the favourite evergreen at both weddings and funerals. There are many varieties, but the species remains the best.

2.0 × 1.5   Well-drained soil   Sun

SALVIA OFFICINALIS COMMON SAGE

The well known dwarf semi-evergreen cultivated as a herb in Britain since the 16th century. The greyish leaves are strongly aromatic, the flowers blue-purple appearing throughout summer. Apart from the commonly known culinary use of sage, it was also used to prevent baldness and to soothe sore throats. These are some good varieties, especially 'Purpurascens' with purple foliage and stems.

0.6 × 0.5   Well-drained   Sun

SAPONARIA OFFICINALIS SOAPWORT OR BOUNCING BET

A naturalized perennial prized by the cottage gardener of old because the glaucous leaves, when crushed, formed a soap-like lather that removed dirt and stains (hence the common name). The white or crimson campion-like flowers appear all summer. There are good doubles, white, pink and crimson-purple. The roots are invasive and it has been described as coarse and untidy – which arguably makes it an ideal candidate for a cottage garden.

0.8 × 0.9   Well-drained   Sun or light shade

SAXIFRAGA × *URBIUM*   LONDON PRIDE
A low, carpeting perennial for the border's edge with rosettes of dark green leaves and dainty sprays of tiny pink flowers from May to July. Grown since earliest times, it was once used for 'breaking up stones in the bladder'.

0.3 × 0.3   Any soil, especially chalk   Partial shade preferred

SCABIOSA   SCABIOUS OR PINCUSHION FLOWER
Very long flowering perennials with frilly-edged pincushion-like flowers, blue or white. *S. caucasica* is the most common species. 'Clive Greaves' is one of the best varieties with pale blue flowers. 'Miss Willmott' is a white. A new scabious, 'Butterfly Blue', is compact and flowering from June to October. There are a number of annual species, including some naturalized such as *S. atropurpurea*.

0.6 × 0.6   Fertile, well-drained, preferably limy   Sun

SYRINGA   LILAC
Hardy deciduous shrubs with high-scented flowers in May and June. *S. vulgaris* is the common species with many named varieties. The flowers are double or single and range in colour from creamy-yellow to red, blue, or purple. It was first introduced in the 16th century. For the cottage garden today it is worth looking beyond this single species of lilac for there are many wonderful types to choose from, for example:
S. × *josiflexa* 'Bellicent' – an outstanding hybrid with fragrant, clear rose-pink flowers.
S. microphylla 'Superba' – a small-leaved shrub seldom taller

than 1.5m with rose pink scented panicles in May and beyond.

S. × *swegiflexa* – strong growth with pink cylindrical flower panicles.

    1.2 to 3.0 × 1.2 to 2.0   Well-drained   Sun or partial shade

THYMUS THYME
A well-known evergreen herb with tiny leaves and purple flowers that are much loved by bees, thyme has been culti-vated since ancient times to flavour food. There are many different species, either creeping or upright in habit. It is ideal for tubs, between paving or at the front of a border.

    0.2 × 0.2   Well-drained especially chalk   Sun

VERBASCUM MULLEIN
Biennial and perennial flowers, usually with large basal leaves and tall, thin spikes of yellow, often furry-edged, flowers. Cottagers would dip these into tallow and burn like a wick for evening light. Most seed themselves with great ease.

V. chaixii – yellow flowers with mauve edges.

V. phoeniceum – short-lived with white, pink or purple flow-ers. One of the parents of the beautiful Cotswold hybrids, which also have various flower colours.

V. olympicum and *V. bombyciferum* – giant biennials with very large grey or silver basal leaves and tall yellow flower spires.

    0.6 to 1.5 × 0.4 to 0.9   Well-drained soil   Sun

VIOLA VIOLET, VIOLA AND PANSY
Another large group of historically important plants. *V. odorata* is the scented sweet violet, cultivated by the ancient Greeks for sweetening purposes. By the Middle Ages its use had greatly expanded and it has been a common sight in cottage gardens since then. The dark violet flowers appear in March and again in autumn. There are pink and white forms and the doubles known as Parma violets.

Viola cornuta – the best of the bunch; a vigorous clump-forming perennial with masses of violet-blue flowers in early summer. 'Lilacina' (pale blue) and 'Alba' are excellent varieties.

Viola tricolor – a biennial, the wild pansy or heartsease loved by country people for hundreds of years and developed into the modern garden pansy in all its many colours and forms.

Some especially beautiful small flowered violas were bred by crossing various species with *V. tricolor* or varieties of it. Fortunately they are still available and sought after today. They include:

'Ardross Gem' – prettily marked blue and yellow.

'Jackanapes' – chocolate-maroon and yellow (named after Gertrude Jekyll's pet donkey).

'Maggie Mott' – large flowers, light mauve in colour.

'Pickering Blue' – sky blue with an orange eye.

All the violas, even the large and winter flowering modern pansy types, look at home in today's cottage garden.

0.1 to 0.3 × 0.3   Well-drained   Sun or light shade

VITIS GRAPE

Deciduous woody climbers. The fruiting types have been grown for wine-making in this country since Roman times. The majority are vigorous enough to climb up a tree or along a pergola or archway. Many species are grown purely for their decorative merits – in particular their autumn foliage tints.

V. 'Brant' – a good compromise: it fruits well and the large leaves turn red-purple and yellow in autumn.

V. vinifera – the original grapevine for wine making. The variety 'Purpurea' has claret-red leaves that turn purple in autumn.

5.0 × 3.0   Any well-drained soil   Sun or part shade

Scabiosa caucasica 'Clive Greaves'

Syringa microphylla 'Superba'

Viola tricolor

Viola cornuta

PLANT CHECKLISTS

··

A FINGERTIP GUIDE TO PLANTS
FOR A DRY GARDEN

There are obviously many plants that suit the cottage garden of today. These lists concentrate on some of the best that are also readily available. Some are old plants traditionally associated with cottage gardens, others are newer but have a cottage garden feel about them. There are no lists of herbs nor fruit as *all* have a place in the cottage garden. However, a few herbs are described in the Directory.

ANNUALS AND BIENNIALS

Plants that live for one or two years for the cottage border. Some are, botanically-speaking, perennials, but, perhaps because they are tender, are usually treated as annuals or biennials. Most of the plants in this list are normally available as seed.

Acroclinium roseum Everlasting HHA
Agrostemma githago Corn Cockle HA
Alcea rosea Hollyhock HB
Amaranthus caudatus Love-lies-
  Bleeding HHA
Anchusa capensis Anchusa HHB
Antirrhinum majus Snapdragon HHA
Bellis perennis Daisy HB
Calendula officinalis Pot Marigold HA
Callistephus chinensis China Aster
  HHA
Campanula medium Canterbury
  Bell HB
Centaurea cyanus Cornflower HA

Clarkia elegans HA
Cobaea scandens Cathedral Bell HHA
Consolida ajacis Annual Larkspur HA
Convolvulus tricolor Morning Glory
  HA
Cosmos bipinnatus Cosmea HHA
Dianthus barbatus Sweet William HB
Dianthus caryophyllus Annual
  Carnation HHA
Digitalis purpurea Foxglove HB
Erysimum cheiri Wallflower HB
Gypsophila elegans Baby's Breath HA
Helianthus annuus Sunflower HA
Helichrysum bracteatum Straw flower
  HHA
Heliotropium peruvianum Heliotrope
  HHA
Ipomoea tricolor Morning Glory HHA
Lathyrus odoratus Sweet Pea HA
Linum grandiflorum Flax HA
Lunaria annua Honesty HB
Matthiola incana Brompton Stock
  HB
Matthiola incana East Lothian Stock
  HHA

Teeming borders in a Dorset cottage garden.

Matthiola incana Ten Week Stock
HHA
Matthiola longipetala subsp. *bicornis*
Night-scented Stock HA
Myosotis alpestris Forget-me-not HB
Nemophila menziesii Baby Blue
Eyes HA
Nicotiana alata Tobacco Plant HHA
Nigella damascena Love-in-a-Mist HA
Papaver nudicale Iceland Poppy HA
Papaver rhoeas Corn Poppy HA
Papaver somniferum Opium Poppy
HA
Reseda odorata Mignonette HA
Scabiosa atropurpurea Sweet
Scabious HA
Silene coeli-rosa Viscaria HA
Tropaeolum majus Nasturtium HA
Verbascum Mullein HB
Viola Pansy, Viola and Violet HA
or HB
Xeranthemum annuum Immortelle
HA

HA – Hardy Annual
HHA – Half hardy Annual
HB – Biennial

HERBACEOUS PERENNIALS FOR THE COTTAGE GARDEN

Achillea Yarrow
Aconitum Monkshood
Ajuga Bugle
Alchemilla mollis Lady's Mantle
Anaphalis Pearly Everlasting
Anchusa Alkanet
Anemone × *hybrida* Japanese
Anemone
Anthemis tinctoria Golden
Marguerite
Aquilegia Columbine
Armeria Thrift
Artemisia Wormwood,
Southernwood etc.
Aster Michaelmas Daisy
Astrantia Masterwort
Brunnera macrophylla Perennial
Forget-me-not
Campanula Bellflower
Catananche caerulea Blue Cupidone
Centaurea Knapweed and
Cornflower
Centranthus ruber Red Valerian
Coreopsis Tickseed

Crambe cordifolia Ornamental Cabbage
Crocosmia Montbretia
Cynara cardunculus Cardoon
Delphinium Delphinium
Dianthus Pink and Carnation
Dictamnus albus Burning Bush
Digitalis Perennial Foxglove
Echinacea purpurea Purple Coneflower
Erysimum Perennial Wallflower
Filipendula ulmaria Meadowsweet
Galega Goat's Rue
Geranium Crane's-bill
Geum Avens
Gypsophila Baby's Breath
Helenium autumnale Sneezeweed
Helianthus Perennial Sunflower
Helleborus Christmas and Lenten Rose
Hemerocallis Daylily
Iris
Leucanthemum maximum Shasta Daisy
Limonium latifolium Sea Lavender or Statice
Linum Perennial Flax
Lunaria rediviva Perennial Honesty
Lupinus Lupin
Lychnis chalcedonica Jerusalem Cross
Lychnis coronaria Dusty Miller
Lychnis flos-jovis Flower of Jove
Lysimachia punctata Yellow Loosestrife
Lythrum salicaria Purple Loosestrife
Monarda didyma Bergamot
Nepeta Catmint
Oenothera Evening Promrose
Paeonia Peony
Papaver orientale Oriental Poppy

Penstemon Penstemon
Phlox
Physostegia Obedient Plant
Platycodon grandiflorus Balloon Flower
Polemonium caeruleum Jacob's Ladder
Polygonatum Solomon's Seal
Potentilla Cinquefoil
Primula Primrose, Cowslip, Auricula etc.
Prunella Self-Heal
Pulmonaria Lungwort
Rudbeckia Coneflower
Salvia Perennial Salvia
Saponaria officinalis Soapwort or Bouncing Bet
Saxifaga × urbium London Pride
Scabiosa caucasica Scabious
Sidalcea Greek Mallow
Sisyrinchium striatum Satin Flower
Solidago Goldenrod
Stachys byzantina Lamb's Tongue
Stachys macrantha Betony
Thalictrum Meadow Rue
Trollius Globe Flower
Verbascum Mullein
Viola Sweet and Horned Violet

SHRUBS AND SUB-SHRUBS FOR THE COTTAGE GARDEN

Abutilon Shrubby Mallow
Amelanchier Snowy Mespilus
Artemisia Wormwood, Southernwood etc.
Atriplex halimus Sea Purslane
Buddleja Butterfly Bush
Buxus Box
Caryopteris Shrubby Verbena
Ceratostigma Hardy Plumbago
Chaenomeles Flowering Quince

Coronilla emerus Scorpion Senna
Corylus avellana Common Hazel
Cytisus Broom
Daphne
Deutzia
Ficus carica Common Fig
Fuchsia
Hebe Shrubby Veronica (some)
Hydrangea (some)
Hyssopus officinalis Hyssop
Kerria japonica Jew's Mallow
Laurus nobilis Bay Laurel
Lavandula Lavender
Lavatera Tree Mallow
Lonicera Shrubby Honeysuckle
Lupinus arboreus Tree Lupin
Myrtus communis Common Myrtle
Perovskia Russian Sage
Philadelphus Mock Orange
Phlomis fruticosa Jerusalem Sage
Phygelius Cape Figwort
Rosmarinus officinalis Rosemary
Santolina Lavender Cotton
Syringa Lilac
Viburnum

FLOWERS OR SEED HEADS FOR DRYING

Achillea Yarrow
Acroclinium roseum Everlasting HHA
Amaranthus caudatus Love-lies-
  Bleeding
Anaphalis Pearly Everlasting
Catananche caerulea Blue Cupidone
Centaurea cyanus Cornflower HA
Cynara scolymus Cardoon
Helichrysum bracteatum Straw
  flower HHA
Humulus Lupulus Hop
Hydrangea
Limonium latifolium Sea Lavender
  or Statice
Nigella damascena Love-in-a-Mist
  HA
Ornamental grasses (annuals and
  perennials)
Papaver Poppy
Sisyrinchium striatum Satin Flower
Xeranthemum annuum Immortelle
  HA

A riotous mix of annuals, perennials, shrubs and trees.

Zéphirine Drouhin.

ROSES FOR A COTTAGE GARDEN

As noted in the Directory, most of what we term the 'old roses' are suitable for inclusion in the cottage garden. Listed here are some of the best – but some further investigation is recommended before you make your final selection.

1. Old Roses

Gallica Roses
'Belle de Crécy'
'Charles de Mills'
R. gallica var. *officinalis*
R. gallica 'Versicolor'

Alba Roses
'Alba Maxima'
'Alba Semiplena'
'Céleste'
'Félicité Parmentier'
'Maiden's Blush'

Damask and Portland Roses
'Mme Hardy'
R. × *damascena* nvar. *semperflorens*
'Portlandica'
R. × *damascena* nvar. *versicolor*

Centifolia Roses
'Fantin-Latour'
R. × centifolia

Moss Roses
R. × *centifolia* 'Muscosa'
'Nuits de Young'
'William Lobb'

Bourbon Roses
'Boule de Neige'
'Louise Odier'
'Mme Isaac Pereire'
'Mme Pierre Oger'
'Souvenir de la Malmaison'

Hybrid Perpetual Roses
'Baronne Prévost'
'Paul Neyron'
'Roger Lambelin'

2. Shrub Roses

Hybrid Musk Roses
'Cornelia'
'Penelope'
'Prosperity'

China Roses
'Cécile Brunner'
R. × odorata 'Pallida' (Old Blush China)

Polyantha Pompon Roses
'The Fairy'
'White Pet'

Modern Shrub Roses
'Lavender Lassie'
'Nevada'
'Yesterday'

3. Species roses and their near relatives

R. elegantula 'Persetosa'

Burnet Roses
R. pimpinellifolia Double White
'Stanwell Perpetual'

English Roses
'Abraham Darby'
'Graham Thomas'
'Heritage'
'Pretty Jessica'

Rugosa Roses
'Agnes'
'Blanc Double de Coubert'

4. Climbing and Rambler Roses
'Albéric Barbier'
'Blairii Number Two'
'Climbing Cécile Brunner'
'Climbing Etoile de Hollande'
'Climbing Pompon de Paris'
'Félicité Perpétue'
Gloire de Dijon
'Rambling Rector'
Rosa filipes 'Kiftsgate'
'Sanders' White Rambler'
'Splendens'
'Zéphirine Drouhin'

5. Modern bedding roses with an old-world feel

H.T. Roses (Large-flowered)
'Golden Melody'
'Shot Silk'

Floribunda (Cluster Roses)
'Iceberg'
'Rosemary Rose'

CLIMBERS FOR A COTTAGE GARDEN

Clematis especially:
C. alpina
C. flammula
C. macropetala
C. montana
C. vitalba
C. viticella
C. rehderiana
Hedera helix Common Ivy and varieties
Humulus lupulus Hop
Jasminum nudiflorum Winter Jasmine
J. officinale Summer Jasmine
Lonicera Honeysuckle
Vitis Grape
Wisteria

TREES FOR A COTTAGE GARDEN

Acer negundo Box Elder
Betula pendula Silver Birch
Cornus mas Cornelian Cherry
Corylus Hazel
Crataegus Thorn
Cydonia oblonga Quince
Ilex aquifolium Holly
Malus Flowering and Fruiting
  Crab Apple
Mespilus germanica Medlar
Morus Mulberry
Prunus avium Gean
Prunus dulcis Almond
Prunus padus Bird Cherry
Prunus × subhirtella Spring Cherry
Pyrus communis Common Pear
Sorbus aucuparia Mountain Ash
Sorbus domestica Service Tree

SCENTED FLOWERS FOR A COTTAGE GARDEN

These are best in a sheltered spot so that the fragrance hangs in the air.

Buddleja Butterfly Bush
C. rehderiana Clematis
Clematis flammula Clematis
Convallaria majalis Lily of the
  Valley
Cytisus Broom
Daphne Daphne
Dianthus Pinks and Carnations
Erysimum cheiri Wallflower
Galtonia candicans Summer
  Hyacinth
Hesperis matronalis Sweet Rocket

Iris Bearded Iris
Jasminum officinale Summer
  Jasmine
Lathyrus odoratus Sweet Pea
Lavandula Lavender
Lilium Lily
Lonicera Honeysuckle
Lupinus arboreus Tree Lupin
Matthiola Stocks
Oenothera Evening Primrose
Paeonia Peony
Philadelphus Mock Orange
Phlox paniculata Perennial Phlox
Reseda odorata Mignonette
Rosa Rose
Syringa Lilac
Viburnum × bodnantense Winter-
  flowering Viburnum
Viola odorata Sweet Violet
Wisteria

CUT FLOWERS FOR THE HOUSE

Most flowers, including those on shrubs and trees, will last at least for a short period in the home. These cottage garden plants are long-lasting and especially recommended:

Alchemilla mollis Lady's Mantle
Antirrhinum majus Snapdragon
Aquilegia Columbine
Callistephus chinensis China Aster
Campanula Bellflower
Centaurea cyanus Cornflower
Consolida Larkspur
Convallaria majalis Lily of the
  Valley
Coreopsis Tickseed

Sisyrinchium striatum Satin Flower
Solidago Goldenrod
Syringa Lilac
Tulipa Tulip
Verbascum Mullein
Viburnum

PLANTS FOR COTTAGE GARDEN CONTAINERS

Any small, compact plant tolerating dryish conditions should do well in a normal-sized container. Listed here is a selection of the best:

Ajuga Bugle
Anemone Windflower
Armeria Thrift
Bellis perennis Daisy
Buxus Box
Calendula officinalis Pot Marigold
Chionodoxa Glory of the Snow
Colchicum Meadow Saffron
Crocus
Cyclamen
Dianthus Sweet William, Pink and Carnation
Fuchsia
Galanthus Snowdrop
Laurus nobilis Bay Laurel
Lavandula Lavender
Lilium Lily
Matthiola Stocks
Muscari Grape Hyacinth
Myosotis alpestris Forget-me-not
Narcissus Daffodil
Nigella damascena Love-in-a-Mist
Primula Primrose, Auricula etc.
Saxifraga × *urbium* London Pride
Tulipa Tulip
Viola Violet, Viola and Pansy

Cosmos bipinnatus Cosmea
Daphne
Delphinium Perennial Delphinium
Dianthus Sweet William, Pink and Carnation
Digitalis Foxglove
Echinacea purpurea Purple Coneflower
Gypsophila Baby's Breath
Hydrangea
Lathyrus Pea
Lavandula Lavender
Leucanthemum maximum Shasta Daisy
Lilium Lily
Lupinus Lupin
Matthiola Stock
Narcissus Daffodil
Paeonia Peony
Penstemon
Philadelphus Mock Orange
Rosa Rose
Scabiosa Scabious

ORNAMENTAL VEGETABLES

Vegetables are traditional components of the cottage garden. The following have particularly decorative parts above ground such as foliage, flowers and/or seed heads and combine well with perennial and annual flowers:

Allium ampeloprasum Porrum Group
  Leek
Allium cepa Onion
Asparagus officinalis Asparagus
Beta vulgaris subsp. *cicla* Swiss
  Chard
Beta vulgaris Crassa Group
  Beetroot
Brassica oleracea Botrytis Group
  Cauliflower
Brassica oleracea Capitata Group
  Cabbage
Brassica oleracea Italica Group
  Sprouting Broccoli
Cichorium endivia Endive
Cichorium intybus Chicory
Cynara cardunculus Cardoon
Cynara scolymus Globe Artichoke
Daucus carota Carrot
Lactuca sativa Lettuce
Phaseolus coccineus Runner Bean
Rheum × *hybridum* Rhubarb
Sanguisorba minor Salad Burnet

PLANTS THAT SELF-SEED

These plants are ideal for the cottage garden, creating a random, informal planting. Annual thinning must be carried out to keep the population under control. Seed of some varieties may not be true, so the resultant plants will be different from the original, but this is perfectly acceptable in the cottage garden.

Alchemilla mollis Lady's Mantle
Aquilegia Columbine
Brunnera macrophylla Perennial
  Forget-me-not
Buddleja Butterfly Bush
Centranthus ruber Red Valerian
Cyclamen
Digitalis purpurea Foxglove
Erysimum cheiri Wallflower
Fritillaria meleagris Snake's-head
  Fritillary
Geranium Crane's-bill
Helleborus Christmas and Lenten
  Rose
Hyacinthoides non-scripta Bluebell
Leucojum Snowflake
Lunaria annua Honesty
Lychnis coronaria Dusty Miller
Matthiola bicornis Night-scented
  Stock
Muscari Grape Hyacinth
Mysotis alpestris Forget-me-not
Nigella Love-in-a-Mist
Oenothera Evening Primrose
Ornithogalum Star of Bethlehem
Papaver Poppy
Primula Primrose etc.
Sisyrinchium striatum Satin Flower
Tropaeolum Nasturtium

Verbascum Mullein (Biennials)
Viola Viola

BULBOUS PLANTS FOR THE COTTAGE GARDEN

Autumn and spring bulbs are especially useful in the cottage garden as they extend the display beyond the summer, with the summer bulbs adding to the main show.

Allium Ornamental Onion
Anemone Windflower
Chionodoxa Glory of the Snow
Colchicum Meadow Saffron
Convallaria majalis Lily of the Valley
Crocus
Cyclamen
Dahlia
Eranthis Winter Aconite
Fritillaria imperialis Crown Imperial
Fritillaria meleagris Snake's-head Fritillary
Galanthus Snowdrop
Galtonia candicans Summer Hyacinth
Hyacinthoides non-scripta Bluebell
Hyacinth
Leucojum Snowflake
Lilium Lily
Muscari Grape Hyacinth
Narcissus Daffodil
Ornithogalum Star of Bethlehem
Puschkinia Striped Squill
Scilla Squill
Tulipa Tulip

Useful Addresses

The Cottage Garden Society,
5 Nixon Lane, Thonhill,
Dewsbury,
West Yorkshire WF12 0JA

Henry Doubleday Research Association, Ryton-on-Dunmore, Coventry CV8 3LG

Hardy Plant Society,
Bank Cottage, Great Comberton,
Worcestershire WR10 3DP

Plants and Seeds

Most garden centres, plant centres and nurseries offer a wide range of suitable plants, but the following companies supply some of the more specialized types:

Mill Cottage Plants,
The Mill, Henley Lane, Wookey,
Somerset BA5 1AP

Cotswold Garden Flowers,
1 Waterside, Evesham,
Worcestershire WR11 6BS

Cottage Garden Plants Old and New, Cox Cottage, Lower Street, East Morden, Wareham, Dorset BH20 7DL

The Cottage Herbery,
Boraston, Tenbury Wells,
Worcestershire WR15 8LZ

Picture Acknowledgements

b–bottom/c–centre/l–left/r–right/t–top

Heather Angel 11(tl)

Bridgeman Art Library 61

Eric Crichton front cover inset, 7, 11(tr), 14, 15, 19(t),
20(tr & bl), 24(b), 25, 26, 27, 29(t), 30, 32, 37(tl), 39(tr), 41(r),
43(tl & cr), 47, 53(tl & cl), 58

Fine Art Photographic/Galerie George 5

Jerry Harpur back cover, 55 (Chiff Chaffs, Bourton, Dorset)

Andrew Lawson 11(b), 17(tl), 19(bl), 24(t), 35, 37(t & b),
43(tr), 53(r)

S. & O. Mathews 39(tl), 40, 41(l), 49

Clive Nichols front cover background, 1, 9, 11(cl), 13, 17(tr & b),
19(br), 20(tl & br), 23, 29(b), 34, 43(b), 44, 53(b), 57

Harry Smith Collection 31